# EXPLORING CELTIC MYTHOLOGY

Don Nardo

San Diego, CA

**For more information, contact:**
ReferencePoint Press, Inc.
PO Box 27779
San Diego, CA 92198
www.ReferencePointPress.com



LIBRARY OF CONGRESS CATALOGING-IN-PUBLICATION DATA

Names: Nardo, Don, 1947- author
Title: Exploring Celtic mythology / by Don Nardo.
Description: San Diego, CA : ReferencePoint Press, Inc, 2026. | Includes bibliographical references and index.
Identifiers: LCCN 2025003167 (print) | LCCN 2025003168 (ebook) | ISBN 9781678210724 library binding | ISBN 9781678210731 ebook
Subjects: LCSH: Mythology, Celtic--Juvenile literature
Classification: LCC BL900 .N38 2026 (print) | LCC BL900 (ebook) | DDC 299/.16--dc23/eng/20250407
LC record available at https://lccn.loc.gov/2025003167
LC ebook record available at https://lccn.loc.gov/2025003168

# Who Were the Celts?

On one side of the battlefield, not far from where the Irish town of Sligo would later rise, stood the Celtic Irish gods, along with the many human warriors who supported them. One of those deities—Brigid, goddess of fire, the hearth, and blacksmiths—stood out as the sun's rays reflected off her gleaming metal armor. Not far from her stood her beloved son, Ruadan, also resplendent in his battle gear.

**Brigid**
The Celtic Irish goddess of fire, hearths, and blacksmiths

Brigid, Ruadan, and their compatriots could see their opponents arrayed in the distance—legions of hideous beings called Fomorians. According to historian Fergus Fleming, "The inhuman wickedness of this monstrous race was represented by their misshapen physical appearance. They were variously described as possessing one leg, one arm, or one eye."[1]

For several minutes the two armies stood still while their members eyed their respective enemies in silence. Finally, the fighters on both sides shouted and charged forward, quickly closing the gap between them. Soon the two armies crashed together and a great bloodletting began. "Great was the slaughter," a surviving medieval text states.

> Abundant was the stream of blood over the white skin of young warriors mangled by the hands of bold men while rushing into danger for shame. Harsh was the noise made by the multitude of warriors and champions protecting their swords and shields and

> bodies while others were striking them with spears and swords. Harsh too was the tumult all over the battlefield—the shouting of the warriors and the clashing of bright shields, the swish of swords and ivory-hilted blades, the clatter and rattling of the quivers, the hum and whirr of spears and javelins, the crashing strokes of weapons.[2]

**Fomorians**
**Misshapen monsters that Celtic myth says occupied Ireland in the dim past**

The gods and their allies eventually won the day and drove most of the Fomorians into the sea. During the victory celebration, however, Brigid received awful news. In the battle, one of the Fomorians had crept up behind brave Ruadan and driven a spear through him, killing him. Hearing this, the grief-stricken Brigid "came and keened [wailed in grief] for her son," the surviving text reads. "At first she shrieked, in the end she wept. Then for the first time weeping and shrieking were heard in Ireland."[3] After that, legends claim, it was the custom of Irishwomen to keen loudly at the graves of dead relatives.

## The Early Celts

This story—with gods, heroes, and a titanic struggle—effectively presents an event related to the supernatural or folklore that supposedly occurred in the real past. But it also has a practical element in that it explains how a common social custom—in this case keening at Irish funerals—came about.

The story of the victory of the gods over the monstrous Fomorians is one of the most often recited and retold myths of one of the world's most colorful past peoples—the Celts. Their exact origins are still somewhat unclear. But modern archaeologists and historians think it is likely that they emerged out of what those experts call the Hallstatt culture. Named after a lake of that name in northern Austria, that society first appeared about 850 BCE. These earliest Celts, mainly farmers and traders, were resilient and hardworking, and their culture thrived in what is now central Europe.

Over time, that success produced consistent population increases. And in turn, it spurred many Celts to migrate outward and even across the sea. Typically, each of these branches of the Celtic tree developed some distinctive local customs. Yet because they were all culturally related, they retained some basic similarities. For instance, all were highly competent metalworkers. In fact, Fleming points out, the Celts "introduced the art of iron forging to Europe and made innumerable agricultural advances—iron plowshares, iron bridle bits, [and] iron tires for their carts. . . . They were [also] accomplished warriors. The same technology that gave them plowshares also provided them with swords, spears, arrows, and, most awe-inspiring of all, iron-wheeled chariots."[4]

## The Last Stronghold

Although Celtic tribes were a strong presence throughout central and northern Europe, the rise of Rome eventually caused their demise. The famous Roman general Julius Caesar decisively de-

*The leader of the Celts throws his weapons at the feet of Julius Caesar after being defeated by him in Gaul.*

feated them in Gaul (what is now France) in the 50s BCE. And most European Celts were thereafter absorbed into Rome's growing empire.

The last major stronghold of the original Celts then became the British Isles, including Wales and Ireland. And that is where the bulk of their lively myths, which for centuries had been passed on solely by word of mouth, were finally written down. Those who performed that task were Christian priests. (The British Celts converted to Christianity between the 400s and 600s CE.) The diligent work of these churchmen ensured that the ancient tales would not disappear altogether. And that turned out to be a source of pride for the descendants of the Celtic bloodline. To a certain extent, Fleming explains, their culture in the British Isles "found a new lease of life, as Christian scribes began to write down the old stories. For the first time, the gods and heroes of Celtic tradition emerged from the shadows. The Celtic spirit, immortalized in figures such as [the heroes] Finn, Cuchulainn, and King Arthur, [now had the chance to live] on."[5]

# Tales of Beginnings

A fateful day in the dimly remembered past began as hundreds and thousands of earlier days had. The pastures and forests of Ireland were mostly brown and brittle from decades in which almost no rain had fallen. Various diseases ran rampant across the land, killing many of the humans, who belonged to a race known as the Fir Bolg. Incessant wars among rival Fir Bolg kings had killed thousands of those who had not died of the plagues. Moreover, an ancient race of nonhuman, monstrous beings called the Fomorians lurked in caves and on remote hillsides; they often raided Fir Bolg villages, stealing and murdering at will.

No one in Ireland knew that on that day of destiny Ireland's chaotic, miserable situation would change for the better. The first portent occurred in the afternoon, when the sun had reached its highest point in the sky. A deafening thunderclap—or at least what sounded like one—rang out, sending powerful shock waves across the land. It was followed by a blinding flash of light, brighter than the sun itself, in the northern sky.

A few minutes later, people across Ireland witnessed an astonishing, seemingly miraculous event. A large, brightly shining hole opened in the northern sky, and from it emerged several hundred human-looking beings. They had no wings, yet they were able to float through the air without falling. Steadily they glided downward until their feet gently touched the ground. And at that moment the spellbound witnesses on farms and in villages saw that these strange visitors were, male and female alike, amazingly beautiful.

Later that afternoon, some local village elders gathered the nerve to approach the visitors and inquire who they were and why they had come. In response, a tall, handsome, bearded man stepped forward. He identified himself as the Dagda, the leader of a race of gods who called themselves the Tuatha De Danann. He himself oversaw fertility and prosperity, he said. Then he introduced some of his fellow deities. Among them were Lugh, god of war; Nuada, who could control the weather; Brigid, goddess of fire, the hearth, and healing; Bodb Derg, god of wisdom; and Oenghus, god of love.

**Lugh**
A member of the Tuatha, he was the Celtic god of war and craft skills

The Tuatha had come from a shadowy, unnamed land lying far to the north, the Dagda explained. Their sacred mission was to rule Ireland and bring health and prosperity back to its people. Although many were receptive to what the Tuatha offered,

*The Fomorians were an ancient race of monstrous creatures that often raided Fir Bolg villages.*

the Fir Bolg king Eochaid mac Eirc was not content to surrender the land. He waged war against the visitors, and in one final bloody battle, the Tuatha emerged victorious. They took control of Ireland, after which the rains returned, and the land became green and prosperous.

## No Traditional Creation Tales

The story of the arrival of the gods—the Tuatha—was among the most beloved and most often recited myths of the Celts who inhabited the British Isles in the medieval era. Members of that society told and retold it, along with other tales about the gods, partly because doing so was entertaining. Yet listening to storytellers recite such myths was also a sort of socially unifying experience.

*Lugh, god or war—shown here beating the Celts' best chess player—was part of a race of gods who called themselves the Tuatha De Danann.*

Indeed, it was a way to keep society cohesive and close-knit. According to historian Barry Cunliffe:

> Listening to the tales of storytellers played a crucial part in everyday life. The stories provided a sense of the inherited past, they informed about the danger and temptations of life, and they provided a set of moral standards that the listener was invited to accept. No less important was the occasion itself—the coming together of family and friends sitting around the hearth engaged in the common pursuit of reflecting on their shared heritage.[6]

In addition to being entertaining and a crucial way to unify Celtic society, the stories about the Tuatha were important because they dealt with the gods' and society's origins. These tales were part of a cycle, or group, of myths that explained not only how the gods arrived but also how the British Isles were supposedly peopled in the first place. It must be stressed that they were not traditional creation stories. That is, they did not explain how the Celts themselves, the world, or humanity came to be.

It is possible, even likely, that such pagan (non-Christian) Celtic creation myths did once exist. If so, they long ago disappeared. The existing Celtic "myths of beginnings," as they are usually called today, are highly Christianized. The Christian priests who committed the myths to paper in early medieval times either destroyed or disregarded any existing pagan creation tales. They then superimposed elements of the Christian creation tales onto old Celtic myths about the earliest inhabitants of the British Isles. As a result, the Celtic tales of beginnings contain a mix of Christian and pagan Celtic elements.

## The First Two Waves of Humans

The cycle of myths about the populating of Ireland and other parts of the British Isles therefore begins with the Christian deity, God, creating the world in six days. A few other traditional biblical tales, including that of Adam and Eve, follow. Of these, the most relevant to Celtic mythology is the story of the great flood, in which Noah and his family survived within a large boat—the ark. A few months before the flood, the Celtic version states, Noah told his granddaughter, Cesair, that she and a few dozen followers might survive if they sailed in three small ships to a distant land called Ireland.

Cesair, accompanied by her father (and Noah's son), Bith, made that voyage and arrived in Connacht, in western Ireland, forty days before the flood. Unfortunately for the band of travelers, Noah had been wrong about their possible survival. On the fortieth day, Luther College professor Philip Freeman writes,

*The story of the flood, where Noah and his family survived within an ark, is one of the biblical tales most relevant to Celtic mythology.*

Bith stood on a mountaintop and "saw the great wall of water coming and knew that he, his daughter, and their people would not survive. The flood overtook Cesair in her valley in Connacht . . . [and] she was the last to die in the mighty deluge that swept the earth."[7]

**Partholonians**
**Led by Partholon, a descendant of Noah, legends claim, they were the second group of humans to settle in Ireland**

For perhaps a century or more after that catastrophe, Ireland remained uninhabited. Then the monstrous, nonhuman Fomorians, who may have originated in the ocean depths, arrived. Two centuries later they witnessed the landing of a second group of humans on the island. The visitors were led by Partholon, a descendant of Noah who had recently established a city in Greece. He and his followers, numbering about one thousand, promptly attacked and defeated the Fomorians, who retreated into some remote hills. The Partholonians proceeded to build towns and introduced farming and sheepherding to Ireland. But after only a few years, they all died from a mysterious plague.

## More Waves of Newcomers

According to the myth of Celtic Irish beginnings, waves of newcomers continued to reach Irish shores. Some thirty years after Partholon and his followers perished, a group of people led by Nemed, another of Noah's early descendants, arrived. They too fought the Fomorians. But this time the monsters won and expelled the surviving Nemedians from the island. Some of those refugees settled in England, while others went to Greece. The Greek Nemedians evolved into the Fir Bolg, who returned to Ireland and seized it from the Fomorians.

The Fir Bolg divided the land into separate realms, each ruled by a king. These rulers fought among themselves for a generation, bringing chaos and misery to most of the island's inhabitants. It was at that pivotal moment in the saga of Celtic beginnings that the sky burst open, and the race of superior beings called the Tuatha arrived on the scene. After defeating the Fir Bolg, the Tuatha brought peace and prosperity to Ireland.

The triumphant gods were successful in part because they possessed numerous magical powers. Despite being divine in certain ways, however, they were not invincible. This was because, unlike the gods of the ancient Greeks and the Christian deity, the Tuatha were not immortal in the physical sense. Rather, the Celtic gods could be killed or die by accident. One saving grace for them, according to legend, was that if they did die, they could return in spirit form. And since those spirits were eternal, later generations of humans could perpetually continue to worship them.

It was partly this vulnerability to physical death that ensured that the Tuatha's reign on earth would be limited. As it turned out, a few centuries after the gods' arrival, a group of Celts known as the Milesians (also called the Gaels) invaded Ireland. These fierce newcomers managed to defeat the Tuatha and drive them from power. Their loss was summed up in an eloquent epitaph by the noted early twentieth-century Irish poet William Butler Yeats. The Celtic gods "are indeed more wise and beautiful than men," he wrote. "But men, when they are great men, are stronger than they are, for men are, as it were, the foaming tide-line of their sea."[8] That is, humans ended up being a powerful wall that encircled and threatened to imprison the Tuatha. With nowhere else to go in the visible world, therefore, the gods retreated into an otherworld. In Celtic lore, such a place is an alternate dimension, an invisible realm that exists, unseen, beside the material world. The Celts came to believe that the otherworld the gods inhabited exists somewhere in the twilight zone between night and day, or between dreaming and waking.

## Bran's Legendary Voyage

The supernatural realm into which the Tuatha withdrew was not the only otherworld described in the collection of tales about Celtic beginnings in the British Isles. There are several others, including the one in the myth of a journey to the mystical Land

## The Death of Monstrous Balor

According to the Celtic myths, during the great battle between the Tuatha and Fomorians, the latter were led by their ruler, Balor. Here, Cardiff University scholar Miranda Aldhouse-Green describes the hideous Balor and how he was killed by the Tuatha war god Lugh.

> The Fomorians had a fearsome champion named Balor. His single eye was so enormous that it took four men to raise the eyelid. When the eye was open, its gaze was so poisonous that . . . it could freeze an entire army in its tracks. No one could survive it. When faced with this awful opponent, Lugh acted swiftly. As soon as Balor's eye swiveled in his direction, he took his sling and aimed straight for it. The force of the sling-stone drove Balor's great eye right through his head, so that it popped out at the back and turned its fatal gaze onto the Fomorians themselves.

Miranda Aldhouse-Green, *The Celic Myths*. London: Thames and Hudson, 2015, p. 68.

of Women. That story—likely dating from 400 CE or earlier—was written down by Irish Christian monks in about 700 CE.

The hero of the story is an Irish Celt—a descendant of the Milesians who took control of the island from the Tuatha. His name was Bran mac Febal. While strolling on a beach one day, he noticed a bough of beautiful flowers lying in the sand. He showed it to some friends, after which they heard a female voice singing a lovely tune. Suddenly, the singer—an unusually attractive woman—appeared. As told by prolific mythologist Arthur Cotterell, she sang "of the great wonders to be found in the lands beyond the sea, the otherworld islands, each larger than Ireland and inhabited by beautiful women who had no knowledge of sorrow, sickness, or death."[9]

The strange woman then vanished. Bran and his companions decided to seek out these faraway isles, a place she had called the Land of Women. The men boarded three ships and headed westward. After seven days, they reached a cluster of islands, and upon going ashore they were greeted by hundreds of beautiful females.

## The Voyage of St. Brendan

Bran's voyage to the legendary Land of Women was the first known example of an old Irish literary form known as *immram*. It consisted of tales of long, daring voyages to distant, unknown, and often mysterious lands. Bran's trip was clearly mythical. But modern historians think it may have been related to a possibly real early medieval journey into the Atlantic Ocean by an Irish churchman named Brendan (later dubbed St. Brendan). One possibility is that Brendan's voyage, if real, inspired the myth of Bran's expedition; the other is that Brendan's trip was inspired by Bran's myth. Supposedly, in about 512 CE Brendan gathered fourteen monks and sailed out into the Atlantic on a journey that took several years. It was said that he found and explored several unknown lands before returning to Ireland. Some scholars suggest that he might have made it to North America, although no direct evidence has yet been found to prove that.

Soon, the male visitors met with the queen of that land. This was indeed the fabled Land of Women, she told them. After urging them to stay as long as they wished, she assigned each man several female guides and servants. A full year elapsed, during which the men enjoyed themselves immensely. Then one of them, Nechtan by name, told Bran that he was homesick and wanted to return to his family in Ireland. Bran polled the others, and they all agreed it was time to head home. Mythologist James Harpur describes what happened next, saying that when Bran's ships reached a western Irish beach,

> a crowd of people shouted out to the ship, asking who they were. Bran bellowed back that he was Bran, son of Febal. The crowd replied that the only Bran they knew of was a character in one of their ancient stories. It was about a man who had set out . . . in search of the Land of Women and had never returned. As it dawned on Bran and his men that they had been away from their homes for centuries, Nechtan leaped from the boat and waded toward the shore. But as soon as he touched dry land, he turned into a pile of ashes.[10]

Bran and the rest of his crew did not desire to suffer Nechtan's fate. So instead of going ashore, they sailed away, never to be seen in Ireland again. Some modern scholars propose that they may have returned to the Land of Women. Or perhaps those voyagers entered a different otherworld described in the tales of Celtic beginnings. If so, Celtic lore supports the notion that Bran and the others still inhabit one of those magical places, along with their reborn comrade Nechtan. Historian Peter B. Ellis explains, "The Celts taught that death is only a change of place and that life goes on, with all its forms and goods, in an other-world. When a soul dies in this world, it is reborn in an otherworld, and when a soul dies in an otherworld, it is reborn in this one."[11]

**Nechtan**

**A sailor who accompanied Bran mac Febal on the voyage to the Land of Women, he convinced Bran to return to Ireland**

# Epic Stories of Lovers

The Irish Celtic god of love, Oenghus, spent several days each week traversing Ireland. One of his two main goals was to do whatever he could to promote loving relationships. Frequently, for instance, he strolled through Irish villages, playing his harp and singing songs that made young adults yearn to fall in love. He did the same across the Irish Sea in Wales, where the locals called him Mabon.

**Oenghus**
**The Celtic Irish god of love**

Oenghus's other chief goal was to help people who were already in love fend off any threats to their happiness. A well-known example was when the beautiful princess Grainne and young warrior Diarmaid fell deeply in love at first sight. They were relentlessly hunted by a powerful military leader who wanted Grainne for himself. Fortunately for the lovers, however, Oenghus covered them with a magical cloak that rendered them invisible to their pursuers.

Even though Oenghus focused on feelings of love between humans, as Fergus Fleming points out, he "himself was not immune to the effects of love."[12] Indeed, one night he had a dream in which a gorgeous maiden told him she adored him. But when he reached out to her, she suddenly disappeared. He continued to have that same dream night after night for an entire year. And the disappointment he felt at never being able to connect with the woman made him increasingly sad.

Hoping to help, Oenghus's father, the Dagda, leader of the Tuatha, initiated a search for the mysterious dream maiden. That quest failed. But a second search led by Oenghus's brother, Bodb Derg, was successful. It turned out that the woman from the dream was a little-known local Irish goddess named Caer. The eager Oenghus tried to approach her and profess his love for her. But for reasons known only to her, she remained aloof.

Eventually, Caer changed her mind and agreed to a meeting. She sent word that Oenghus should meet her on the shore of a lake in central Ireland. Hurrying there, the love god saw 150 swans swimming in the water. One of them called out to him, revealing that Caer had transformed herself into a swan. Oenghus now wasted no time in turning himself into a swan so that he could approach her on equal terms. According to Fleming, "The couple embraced and swam round the lake three times, consummating their love as they did so. They then flew away to Oenghus's home at Newgrange [in eastern Ireland]. Once there, they regained human form and held a great feast, at which they both sang so beautifully that all their guests were lulled to sleep for three days and nights."[13]

## Intense Emotions and Obsessive Behavior

The strange but charming story of how Oenghus and Caer met and professed their love for each other is only one of many tales of love and lovers in the annals of Celtic mythology. These myths vary considerably in their content, tone, and outcomes. In some, love is portrayed as a constructive force that brings about positive results for the lovers. In other Celtic stories, the initial loving relationships break down under the weight of jealousy, betrayal, or revenge.

Thus, in the Celtic myths, love emerges as a complex force that cannot be easily influenced or managed, even by the gods. The love affairs in those tales tend to involve intense emotions and obsessive behavior and often have tragic outcomes. As Robert Seutter, an expert on Celtic mythology, puts it, "One of the things you notice when you read about 'love done Celtic' is that it

*One night Oenghus had a dream in which a gorgeous maiden told him she adored him.*

is epic." Early Celtic storytellers, he points out, wrote "love stories as if love is beautiful, terrible, and unstoppable. . . . [In those tales] getting smitten with love was a force of nature, akin to being hit by a freight train, and it usually ended badly."[14]

## A Beautiful Maiden Reborn

One famous Celtic love story that ends on a happy rather than sad note is that of Midir, one of the Dagda's sons, and Etain, a beautiful young Irishwoman. One day the two, who had never met, passed each other on a country road. Unexpectedly, when they gazed at each other, they fell instantly in love. Midir and the maiden strongly desired to be together, but Midir told her it would be difficult and perhaps even dangerous. The problem was that he was already married to a minor goddess named Fuamnach, who was also a witch adept at casting spells.

Midir's worry proved justified. Although he and Etain tried to keep their mutual love secret, Fuamnach soon found out. Wracked with jealousy, she inflicted Etain with an enchantment that transformed her into a fly. The witch also conjured up a windstorm that carried the fly high into the sky, where it was buffeted helplessly in the upper atmosphere for several years. Eventually, as Philp Freeman tells it, the bedraggled fly "landed on a ceiling pole in the house of Etar, a warrior from Ulster. She fell from the ceiling into a gold cup held by the wife of Etar, so that the woman swallowed [her] unaware. The wife of Etar then conceived a child in her womb and bore a girl nine months later. Etar gave the name Etain to the child and welcomed her into his home."[15]

In the meantime, while the reborn Etain was growing up, the distressed Midir relentlessly searched for his missing lover. When he finally found her, she was a young adult who had recently married a powerful Irish king named Eochy. Entering Eochy's palace, called Tara, Midir found Etain, took her aside, and identified himself. To his dismay, however, she had no recollection of him. Forlorn but undaunted, he proceeded to tell her about her past and urged her to leave with him immediately. Still, however, he was unable to jog her memory, so in a fit of desperation, he seized her and kissed her on the lips. At this, her eyes widened, and her body trembled as she abruptly remembered every moment of her former life.

With her memories restored, the young woman now agreed to leave with her soulmate. At that moment, however, Eochy and several of his soldiers appeared and rushed toward the couple. What they had not counted on was Midir's divine powers, including the ability to transform himself and others into animal form. In

*As the soldiers rushed towards them, Etain and Midir rose up into the air.*

the words of popular Irish playwright and storyteller Sam McBratney, Eochy and his men were astounded to see "Etain and Midir rise into the light streaming from a great window near the roof. Then Eochy [cried aloud] and raced outside. With his warriors round about him . . . he looked up and saw two swans together flying eastward from Tara."[16]

## Culhwch's Love for Olwen

Another tale of romance involves a handsome young warrior named Culhwch. He was the son of the legendary Welsh king, Cilydd. Unfortunately, Culhwch's mother died when he was a boy, and his father married again. What no one in the realm realized at the time was that Culhwch's stepmother was a powerful witch with a nasty temper. When the young man reached his early twenties, the queen tried to persuade him to marry her daughter, his stepsister. But he cared little for the stepmother and even less for her daughter, so he declined the marriage offer.

**King Cilydd**
**The father of the hero Culhwch, lover of the maiden Olwen**

Furious at this refusal, the stepmother cast a debilitating spell on Culhwch. It made him desperately want to court and marry only one woman—a gorgeous maiden named Olwen. What made this a perilous curse was that her father was Ysbaddaden, a monstrous and mean-spirited giant who had vowed to keep her unwed.

The charmed Culhwch therefore faced the dilemma of how to obtain access to Olwen without raising her father's ire. When the young man went to the king to seek guidance, Cilydd reminded him that the most famous and powerful ruler in the British Isles—King Arthur—was a close family relation. According to Peter B.

## Swans: A Celtic Symbol

**As depicted in the tales of Midir and Etain, Oenghus and Caer, and some other myths from the ancient British Isles, swans made frequent appearances in Celtic mythology. Cardiff University scholar Miranda Aldhouse-Green here explains the potent symbolism of swans in Celtic society and myths.**

> Swans are charismatic birds: large, white, beautiful, and sometimes fierce, although often seen swimming serenely on the calm surface of the water. Waterfowl possessed powerful symbolism in Celtic myths because they are at home in all elements: water, air, and land. The dazzling plumage of swans perhaps gave them an extra edge, as it evoked purity; and their monogamous habit of pairing for life made them icons of faithful and enduring devotion, highly appropriate for divine lovers. Storytellers gave swans a much better press than their antitheses [opposites], the crow and the raven, black carrion birds that often foretold disaster and picked over the slain on the battlefield.

Miranda Aldhouse-Green, *The Celic Myths*. London: Thames and Hudson, 2015, p. 72.

Ellis, Cilydd told Culhwch, "Go to your cousin, the mighty Arthur. As your cousin, he is bound to offer you gifts. Ask of him the gift of delivering Olwen to you."[17]

The lovesick Culhwch took this advice and approached his cousin, who lived in the stately castle of Camelot. Agreeing to help, Arthur ordered three of his knights to accompany Culhwch to Ysbaddaden's mansion. Upon arriving there, the four men diligently searched the area, and one of the knights found a local female goat herder who was acquainted with Olwen. The herder said she was happy to help, and later that day she met secretly with Olwen and set up an equally secret rendezvous between her and Culhwch.

That meeting turned out to be pivotal. The minute that Olwen looked upon her ardent young suitor, she fell in love with him. She advised Culhwch to go to Ysbaddaden and agree to do whatever he demanded in exchange for permitting the marriage to happen. Culhwch did that, and sure enough, the giant said he would consent to the marriage if the young man accomplished a series of extremely difficult tasks. The most challenging one, Ysbaddaden stated, was for Culhwch "to go to the great forest that lies to the

## A Matter of Time

**One of the most famous, and saddest, of the many Celtic love stories is that of Oisin and Niamh. Oisin was a heroic warrior, and Niamh was a princess of Land of the Young, one of the several Celtic otherworlds. They met and fell in love when she visited Ireland for a few weeks. Though smitten with her, Oisin felt it was strange that she refused ever to climb down from her horse. At the end of her stay, she asked him to return with her to her homeland, and he did. There they wed and lived happily for three years. Then Oisin asked if he could pay a short visit to Ireland to visit his father. She assented but warned him to stay always mounted on the horse she would provide for the journey. Arriving at his home village, the young man was shocked to find that his father had been dead for three centuries. Now Oisin realized that for each year he had spent in Niamh's world, a century had passed in Ireland. The next day, he accidentally fell from the horse. Within minutes he transformed into an elderly man and died before he could attempt to return to his wife.**

east. Cut down the trees, plow the land, and sow it with wheat, and, out of the wheat, bake bread for the wedding guests. That task must be done in a single day."[18]

Clearly, Ysbaddaden assumed that the young man would fail to do that and the other tasks. But to the giant's utter surprise, Culhwch managed to complete them all. Enraged, Ysbaddaden shouted that he had changed his mind. No matter what Culhwch did, there would be no marriage. Hearing this, the young man decided there was no other choice but to kill Ysbaddaden, and after a brief but bloody fight, the giant lay dead on the ground.

When Culhwch, accompanied by Olwen, returned to his homeland, he found that his father, stepmother, and stepsister had all died in his absence. That meant that Culhwch was now king and Olwen was his queen. Thereafter, to the delight of the local citizenry, Ellis writes, the two "ruled the land wisely and justly, and lived happily for the rest of their lives."[19]

## Deirdre's Sad but Compelling Tale

Although the tales of Midir and Etain and Culhwch and Olwen end on a positive note, many of the Celtic love stories end tragically. Perhaps the saddest of them all is that of a young Irishwoman named Deirdre, often called Deirdre of the Sorrows. When she was born in Ulster, in northern Ireland, a religious leader announced a prophecy about her. This prediction claimed that she would obtain wondrous beauty but that men's desire for her would cause the death of many Ulster warriors. A number of those fighters therefore wanted to kill her before she grew up.

**Naoise**

**A warrior who falls in love with Deirdre of the Sorrows**

However, Ulster's king, Conchobar, protected Deirdre, selfishly saving her so that he could eventually marry her, Ireland's most beautiful woman. Unknown to the king, when she reached her late teens, she met a warrior from central Ireland named Naoise. The

*King Conchobar takes Deirdre back to Ulster after killing her lover Naoise.*

two fell in love and eloped to Scotland. But the angry Conchobar tracked them down and ordered his warriors to kill Naoise.

Shattered with grief, Deirdre was dragged back to Ulster. There, Conchobar saw that she was overcome with sorrow over her lover's demise. Irritated by that, the king decided to punish her before marrying her. But she would have none of it. One day when the two were standing in his moving chariot, she threw herself to the ground, where her head was crushed by a stone.

The late, noted American mythologist Charles Squire called Deirdre's myth the most often retold of the Celtic love stories. He added that no other past people produced tales so sad and yet so compelling as those of the Celts. These stories, he said, "have a romantic beauty found in no other early literature."[20]

# The Great Celtic Heroes

Although most of the heroes of Celtic mythology were male, a few were female. And one of the hallmarks of those remarkable women was the courage they displayed in standing up to the powerful men who controlled that decidedly male-dominated society. Of those women, who over time became household names in Ireland, Wales, and other parts of the British Isles, none were better known or more respected than Macha.

Macha's story began when a strong but selfish and tyrannical man named Conchobar ruled Ulster. One day one of his nobles, Cruinniuc, a widower with several sons, came home from a walk and found a beautiful woman standing near his house. Introducing herself simply as Macha, she walked inside and took charge of the place. From that time on, to Cruinniuc's puzzlement but also his delight, she became his lover, housekeeper, cook, and mother figure for his sons. Not only did she excel at all these duties, but she was also so swift a runner that she could chase down the fastest deer in Ulster's forests.

**Macha**

**An Irishwoman who became a heroic role model in part because she could outrun galloping horses**

Two years later, Cruinniuc attended a public festival that included feasts and athletic games. He wanted to bring Macha, by now officially his wife, with him. But she chose to stay home because she was nine months pregnant and due to go into labor at any moment. At the festival, Cruinniuc saw that the traditional chariot race, which almost every year King Conchobar's team won, was about to start. Professor Philip Freeman says that in a moment of genuine pride, Cruinniuc told a friend, “My wife can run even faster than the king’s horses.”[21] Unfortunately for Cruinniuc, one of Conchobar’s soldiers overheard that remark and dragged him to the king’s tent. There, Conchobar demanded that Cruinniuc back up his outrageous claim and sent soldiers to fetch Macha. She objected, pointing out that she was pregnant. But a soldier informed her, “If you don’t come, your husband will die.”[22]

By the time Macha stood before the king, her labor pains had begun. Yet he cruelly ordered her to enter the race on foot. Reluctantly, she agreed to do it. But she also uttered a curse, saying that “a great evil will come upon Ulster because of this.”[23]

*After King Conchobar forced her to run in the chariot race, Macha cursed the men of Ulster.*

In the moments that followed, everyone present witnessed something so extraordinary that they were fated to remember it for the rest of their lives. As the horse-drawn chariots sped around the track, the pregnant but fantastically fleet-footed Macha caught up to and finally surpassed them. Having won the race, she laid down on the track and delivered twins—a boy and a girl. To commemorate her incredible victory, a few years later Ulster's capital was given the name Emain Macha, meaning "Twins of Macha."

Moreover, Macha's curse came to pass. "For nine generations," Freeman writes, "whenever danger came upon the province, all the men of Ulster would collapse in labor pains, unable to move in their agony."[24] The talented and heroic Macha had demonstrated to Irish Celts, along with Celts everywhere, that though men remained largely in political control, women were a force to be reckoned with in society.

## A Fascination for Heroes

Macha's tale, together with those of her many male counterparts—Cuchulain, Finn MacCool, Culhwch, and others—make up a huge segment of Celtic mythology. The reason for this is that as a people, the Celts were particularly enthralled by stories about heroic people and events. Indeed, the exploits of such physically attractive and fearless men and women were told and retold for centuries, at first by word of mouth and later in written accounts. Those heroic tales, says Aimee Vipond, who has extensively retold them online, "are replete with stories of epic battles, personal sacrifices, and heroic quests that test the limits of courage. Bravery is frequently portrayed as a necessary quality for leaders and warriors alike. . . . These narratives not only celebrate individual acts of bravery but also highlight the collective spirit of the Celtic people, encouraging a sense of unity and resilience."[25]

Modern mythologists think that this fascination for heroes may have been based on how the Celts viewed themselves, or at least the most outstanding individuals among them. The mythical heroes were typically exceedingly courageous, were skilled in

## An Ideal Patriotic Figure

For many centuries Cuchulain has been the favorite hero, as well as by far the most popular character, in Celtic Irish mythology. Moreover, he has also been highly influential socially and politically. In particular, he has often appealed to the Irish people's sense of nationalism, or their deep feelings of patriotism for their country. At first, in the early medieval era, such feelings were confined mainly to the residents of Ulster, where the myths say Cuchulain was born. Over time, however, his popularity spread over all of Ireland. And even in modern times, his influence as an ideal patriotic figure remained strong. In the twentieth century, for example, when Irish rebels fought to gain independence from Britain, spokesmen for their cause sometimes invoked his name. Typically, they called on Irish people everywhere to remember the mighty "Hound of Ulster" and his tireless defense of his homeland. Indeed, despite Cuchulain being a mythical figure, thousands of Irish rebels identified with him because he was said to have fought and died for the same thing they were fighting for—Irish freedom.

warfare, and had a strong sense of fairness and justice. In Celtic eyes, therefore, the legendary heroes reflected an ideal vision of what society could be at its best. In a sense, scholar Christopher R. Fee suggests, such heroes were, "in effect, Everyman," or what the average Celt aspired to be. A hero's "trials, tribulations, battles, and journeys of growth and transformation mirrored [the ordinary individual's] own innermost fears, desires, and needs."[26]

In addition, heroes appealed so much to the Celts because their daring deeds and emotional struggles were entertaining. The custom of storytelling was deeply imbedded in Celtic culture. The society had few or no books, and as was common in all early civilizations, heroic stories were easy to spread by word of mouth. And the art of good storytelling provided much needed relief from the drudgery and sometimes monotony of everyday life.

## Culain's Hound

Not only in the ancient and medieval eras but also today, one Celtic hero stands out among all the others. An Irish national hero of epic proportions, his birth name was Setanta. But he was and remains far better known as Cuchulain, meaning "Hound of Culain," a nickname he earned in his youth.

**Culain**
**The finest blacksmith in Ulster, after whom the great hero Cuchulain was named**

Not long after Setanta was born in the northern Irish kingdom of Ulster, his mother, Dechtire, noticed that the boy grew faster and was considerably stronger than other small children. That trend continued, and by age five he was twice as strong as an average adult male. He was also more mature and ambitious than most grown-ups, which motivated him to seek an audience with Ulster's ruler, Conchobar.

Astounded by the boy's strength, resolve, and uncommon boldness, the king invited Setanta to train with the realm's leading warriors. Conchobar explained that he needed as many capable fighters as he could find. This was because Ulster was consistently under attack by the army of Connacht, a kingdom lying southwest of Ulster.

Not long after the boy began his training, the kingdom's leading blacksmith, Culain, held a party for the king. Thinking all the guests had arrived, per his usual routine Culain placed his large guard dog, Halfwolf, outside the front door. What the man did not realize was that one guest, young Setanta, was late. And when the boy arrived, Halfwolf did its duty and lunged at him. In an instant, the youngster grabbed the spear he always carried on his back, jabbed it into the canine's chest, and lifted the massive beast into the air. As Sam McBratney tells it, the warriors inside the house heard Halfwolf's high-pitched screams and hurried to the front door. There, "they saw the dog in the air above Setanta's head as he flung it against the pillar of the gate. It slumped to the ground in a limp heap. Even as it struggled to its feet again, Setanta thrust his javelin into its body, and it lay quite still."[27]

The burly blacksmith was glad that the boy had survived, but he was also quite naturally dismayed over the loss of his trusty dog. His only other hound, he explained, was still too young to

*After Halfwolf lunged at him, Setanta grabbed his spear and thrust it into the animal.*

guard the house. Hearing this, with an amazing display of decency and fairness, Setanta apologized and added, "While the pup is growing, I will take Halfwolf's place. I will protect your property and your animals until the pup is old enough to do the job."[28] True to his word, the boy stood outside the house through many a long night in the cold, and in the rain as well, until the other dog took his place. One day, in friendly jest, someone called him Culain's hound, and the name stuck.

## Hymn to a Fallen Champion

In the years that followed, Cuchulain became the mightiest warrior Ireland had ever seen. People were awestruck by him for his unmatched fighting skills, as well as the fact that he seemed to possess certain magical traits. The most impressive one was the incredible transformation he underwent shortly before entering battle. Some called it the "battle frenzy," and others the "killing trance" or "warp spasm." One medieval document states that that scary physical alteration turned Cuchulain

> into a monstrous thing, hideous and shapeless, unheard of. His shanks [limbs] and his joints, every knuckle and angle and organ from head to foot, shook like a tree in the flood or a reed in a stream. His body made a furious twist inside his skin, so that his feet and shins and knees twitched to the rear and his heels and calves switched to the front [and] he sucked one eye [deep] into his head [and] the other eye fell out along his cheek. His mouth weirdly distorted [and] his lungs and liver flapped in his mouth and throat.[29]

Thanks to the fantastic creature lurking inside him, Cuchulain helped Ulster win innumerable battles. But it turned out that this seemingly invincible fighter was not destined to live a long life. When he was seventeen, he faced his biggest and final challenge when Medb, queen of Connacht, marched an enormous army into Ulster. At that time, all of Ulster's other soldiers were unable to fight because of a curse recently placed on them by an angry goddess. So Cuchulain had to face Medb's huge host alone. And in an amazing display, he slew hundreds of enemy warriors each day.

The problem for the young champion was that he never had a chance to rest. Medb kept sending her troops at him in one attack after another, and in each of those encounters, he sustained serious wounds. Finally, he could no longer repel the oncoming soldiers, who managed to cut him to pieces. Mere minutes later, however, Ulster's stricken warriors broke free of the curse, poured onto the battlefield, and slaughtered the invaders. The victors then sang a hymn of praise for their fallen champion. By buying them precious time, they said, he had saved Ulster from annihilation.

## The Band of Ethical Heroes

Another Celtic hero whom the Irish immortalized in myths was the great warrior Fionn mac Cumhaill, often rendered in English as Finn MacCool. Ancient Irish tales say that his birth name was Demne. Supposedly, as a young man he took the name Finn, meaning "fair," because his skin was unusually pale.

> ***fiana***
> Also called the Fenians, the band of ethical warriors led by Finn MacCool

Finn's wide-ranging renown in Celtic Irish mythology is largely based on his effective leadership of a band of valiant, adventurous young men known as the *fiana*, or Fenians. They were said to roam through Ireland, as well as parts of nearby Scotland. Each Fenian was brave, an excellent hunter and warrior, a fighter for justice, and a well-educated scholar or poet.

Now and then, Finn and his men fought for one local king or another. But more often they took it upon themselves to defend the Irish Celts against attacks by outside intruders, including Viking raiders from Scandinavia and even monsters such as giants and trolls. Charles Squire wrote that the Irish "have always held

### Finn and the Salmon of Knowledge

Several quaint myths have survived about Finn MacCool, leader of the brotherhood of heroes known as the Fenians. One of these tales explains how he obtained one of his many constructive skills—the ability to store and recall enormous amounts of factual knowledge. When he was a boy, the story goes, his mother wanted him to have the best education possible. So she hired a private tutor for him, a religious leader named Finegas. Finn was eager to learn new things and had an excellent memory, so Finegas told him about a special, little-known kind of fish—the Salmon of Knowledge. After cooking and eating one, the young man felt a tremendous quantity of knowledge flowing into his mind. And for the rest of his life, he was able answer almost any question about animals, plants, and other aspects of the natural world. Thanks to this simple myth, succeeding generations of Irish Celts came to call fish "brain food." That casual cultural expression survived into modern times and remains common today in English-speaking countries, including the United States.

*Finn MacCool (center) was a famous Irish hero who fought with other warriors, as shown here, to protect Ireland.*

that the Fenians were a kind of native militia, and that Finn was their general."[30]

Moreover, the *fiana* set a sort of ethical standard for the medieval and early modern Irish. According to legend, for instance, Finn swore never to refuse hospitality to anyone in need and never to insult any woman. Over the centuries numerous Irish parents, soldiers, and political leaders have sought to emulate such commitment to decency and honor.

Furthermore, many generations of Irish came to believe that Finn and his followers never actually died. Instead, the legend claims, they remained alive in an ancient otherworld. Like other renowned Celtic heroes of old, British scholar Anne Ross says, "There they lie to this day, fast asleep with their horses and their weapons beside them, until they are awakened by the sound of trumpets proclaiming that their beloved country is in danger. Then they will rise again in the full strength of their valor . . . to defend their people as they did in days gone by."[31]

# Strange Creatures and Scary Monsters

Long ago, in a half-forgotten age, the region of northern Ireland in and around the town of Dungiven was terrorized by a person who had returned from the grave. He also sustained himself on human blood, which in modern terms made him a vampire. In life, he had been a local chieftain named Abhartach. Even before he had gained power, there had been disturbing rumors claiming he was an evil wizard possessing magical abilities. Most people in the region therefore feared him.

The story goes that over time, Abhartach came to suspect his wife was cheating on him. So one day, intending to spy on her, he climbed up on a high ledge near a window of her bedchamber. Somehow, he lost his footing and fell more than 40 feet (12 m) to the stone pavement below. Some of his advisors hurried to the scene and found him dead. Dutifully, they buried their chieftain standing up (a custom afforded to political leaders at the time) in the graveyard of a local church.

That should have been the end of Abhartach's story. But it was not. The very next day a farmer who lived near the church was found dead, his blood having been drained, and witnesses said they saw Abhartach stooping over the victim's body. The assumption was that the former chieftain had used black magic to conquer death. Understandably terrified, the locals sent word to the chieftain of a neighboring region that they needed his help. This chieftain, Cathan,

**Cathan**

An Irish hero who tracked down and slew the vampire known as Abhartach

was widely known as a skilled, heroic, and fearless warrior who had dedicated himself to protecting his subjects from harm.

Wasting no time, as soon as he arrived in Dungiven, Cathan tracked down the undead creature, hacked off its arms, and watched it bleed out. Certain it was dead, he buried the remains in the same churchyard, after which he stayed the night at a local inn. It turned out to be a good thing he remained in Dungiven, because the next morning another

*After discovering Abhartach's new grave empty and realizing that the vampire had revived itself again, Cathan sought the advice of a local pagan priest, as pictured here.*

## A Scary Yet Tragic Tale

Some people today feel that the story of the Celtic female vampire, Dearg Due, is almost as tragic as it is scary. This is because of the terrible mistreatment she endured in human form. According to the tale, she started out as a beautiful, kind young woman who lived in the southern Irish town of Waterford. When she was in her late teens, she fell in love with a handsome, personable young farmworker. But her father forbade her from marrying a poor laborer and instead forced her to wed a much older, well-to-do landowner. The husband was extremely cruel and regularly beat her because he enjoyed seeing people suffer. Miserable, she daydreamed about her former boyfriend arriving to save her. But he never came, and eventually she grew horribly thin and weak and finally died. Her husband refused even to bury her, so a group of sympathetic local villagers performed that kindness. What happened next surprised everyone. During the night following the funeral, her spirit became so angry that it refused to rest peacefully. Taking material form as a bloodthirsty vampire, the creature killed both the boy's father and her husband and drained them of their blood. That act gave the vengeful spirit a strong taste for blood, and in the years that followed, Dearg Due killed many more people.

farmer was found dead, his body having been drained of blood. Cathan checked Abhartach's new grave and, finding it empty, realized that the vampire had somehow revived itself again.

This time the visiting chieftain wisely sought the advice of a local pagan priest. Known for his knowledge of witches, demons, and other evil beings, the holy man said there was only one way to kill an undead bloodsucker like Abhartach. Namely, one must stab it in the heart with a stake cut from a yew tree, place the body upside down in a deep hole in the ground, and cover the grave with branches from an ash tree.

Expressing thanks for this valuable information, Cathan once more tracked down the vampire. This time the hero followed the procedure the priest had described, and the vampire's fate was sealed. In the years that followed, no one in or near Dungiven was murdered and drained of their blood.

## A Deep Connection to Animals

Although Abhartach had been eliminated, local legends claim that other vampires roamed through ancient and medieval Ireland. Perhaps the most infamous was a female bloodsucker known as Dearg Due (meaning "Red Thirst"). It was said that she killed many people around Waterford in southern Ireland.

These deadly menaces were not the only bizarre beings that supposedly plagued the residents of early Ireland and the other British Isles. Mythical Celtic lore is filled with tales of other weird creatures and monsters. Some, including leprechauns (small goblins said to hoard coins and gold) and the pooka (a shape-shifting fairy), were merely strange or mischievous. Although troublesome at times, they were not usually dangerous. Other creatures, however, among them redcaps (murderous goblins) and the Ellen Trenchend (a three-headed, flying dragon), were quite lethal.

It is only natural to wonder why Celtic mythology features so many colorful creatures and monsters. Cardiff University scholar Miranda Aldhouse-Green points out that those strange beasts are often a mixture of the aspects of real animals and various mystical, unreal qualities. In fact, she says, inventing such creatures was natural because Celtic society had a deep connection to animals as well as a strong belief in magic and the otherworldly. She continues:

> Real animals are a deeply important part of the human experience and monstrous beings are combinations of the real and the imagined, the stuff of nightmares and dreams. . . . Monsters are necessary for human society [to keep its collective imagination alive]. In our own day, fascinated by space and the possibility of worlds beyond, we conjure up fantastic images of galactic monsters [that invade Earth].[32]

Historical writer Cierra Tolentino adds that the myths about monsters had a specific function in Celtic society. "More often than not," she says, "they act as a warning . . . especially [to] children, who are the unfortunate targets of many frightening tales."[33] That is, the Celts took the bogeyman concept—that a scary monster would punish disobedient children—to an extreme. Tolentino makes the point that instead of a single bogeyman, Celtic society had many.

## A King's Wish Is Granted

Of those bogeymen, one of the less frightening, though still creepy, was the leprechaun. In some myths leprechauns were categorized as fairies; in others they were goblins or elves. However they were described, they were commonly very small in stature. These creatures were portrayed as mischievous and obsessed with collecting and guarding caches of treasure. Indeed, in exchange for a valuable item, leprechauns would often grant wishes (in most stories, three wishes) to humans.

Such wish granting appears in one of the most often retold tales of those "wee folk," as the Irish still call them. Following a military campaign, the story goes, an early Irish king named

## The Celtic Practical Joker

One of the more colorful creatures found in the collected Celtic myths is a kind of fairy known as a pooka. Part of what made it so intriguing is that, according to modern mythologists, it was one of the most accomplished shape-shifters in world mythology. Its natural shape was somewhat horselike, but a pooka could quickly transform itself into a cow, horse, dog, cat, goat, donkey, wolf, fox, rabbit, frog, or even bird or insect. It could also make itself look like a human being. Whatever form a pooka chose to adopt, often it enjoyed causing mischief. One of its favorite practical jokes was to transform into a large horse and lure an unwitting person, most often someone who was intoxicated, into mounting it and going for a ride. Once on the creature's back, the person was in for a wild, at times unnerving, journey that could last several hours. Only rarely did the victims of such a trick suffer permanent harm, however. In fact, some pookas admired humans and tried to help them. There were even scattered claims that pookas aided farmers in harvesting crops.

Fergus was captured by a group of leprechauns while he was sleeping. Intending to make some money by holding him for ransom, they lugged him toward their home.

Eventually, the kidnappers reached a wide stream. As they carried the man across, one of his feet touched the water, which awakened him. Quickly, he gained his footing, grabbing hold of three of the leprechauns in the process. The tables now turned, they begged him to release them, but he refused. Only if they granted him a wish, he said, would he let them go. When they asked what that wish was, he replied that he desired a magic charm that would allow him to breathe underwater. The three sprites granted the wish, and for the rest of his life, Fergus was able to walk along the sea bottom without drowning.

## A Starving Man and a Screaming Woman

Another eerie mythical Celtic creature was the so-called Fear Gorta, or "hungry man." According to legend, he appeared only in times of famine and would wander through the countryside begging for scraps of food. Descriptions of him claimed he was abnormally thin, clearly from starvation, and had light green skin. Supposedly, people who gave him food or a place to sleep for the night enjoyed unusually good luck in the years that followed. Conversely, those who refused to help him might experience some bad luck, but there were no reports of him physically harming anyone.

**Fear Gorta**
The so-called hungry man who, during times of famine, wandered the countryside and asked for handouts of food

More frightening than the Fear Gorta, but also largely harmless, was one of the most famous of all the Celtic creatures. The Irish called it the banshee; in Scotland it was known as the *bean nighe*, and the Welsh knew it as the *cyhyraeth*. Essentially, it was a female being who foretold of the impending death of a family's loved one. That warning came in the form of a loud, grief-stricken wail. The popular nineteenth-century English Irish folklorist Lady

*The banshee was a famous Celtic creature that foretold of the impending death of a family's loved one.*

Jane Wilde composed a memorable description of a typical banshee, saying that sometimes it

> assumes the form of some sweet-singing virgin of the family who died young, and has been given the mission by the invisible powers to become the harbinger [herald] of coming doom to her mortal kindred. Or she may be seen at night as a shrouded woman, crouched beneath the trees, lamenting with a veiled face; or flying past in the moonlight, crying bitterly. And the cry of this spirit is mournful beyond all other sounds on earth, and betokens [indicates] certain death to some member of the family whenever it is heard in the silence of the night.[34]

## Monsters with Black Hides and Red Hats

Leprechauns, the hungry man, and the banshee were undoubtedly weird creatures. Their one saving grace, some mythologists point out, is that they were not bloodthirsty monsters. However, the Celtic myths did have their share of such lethal beings.

One of the scariest of the mythical Celtic monsters was the kelpie, a water creature said to haunt Irish and Scottish lakes and ponds. What made kelpies particularly dangerous was that they were shape-shifters. In their normal form they resembled jet-black horses having mouths filled with big, sharp teeth. But they could quickly transform themselves into any form they chose. It was said to be common, for instance, for kelpies to become handsome men. In that guise, legends claim, they lured women away from their families. Once alone with such a victim, the monster changed back to its natural form and dragged her into the water, where it drowned and devoured her.

*Kelpies were water creatures and in their natural form they resembled horses.*

Several myths involving kelpies describe them as being especially fond of eating children. In one tale, a kelpie kept its equine form but was careful to hide its sharp teeth. After making itself appear to be equipped with a saddle and bridle, it approached a little girl and asked whether she would like to go for a ride. She said yes. And as soon as she mounted the beast, her fingers stuck fast to its mane, making it impossible for her to climb off. The creature then dove into the water, carrying her to certain death.

Among the other deadly inhabitants of the mythical Celtic bestiary were the redcaps. The late, popular English folklorist William Henderson described one of them, saying that it looked like "a short thickset old man, with long prominent teeth." The typical redcap also possessed "skinny fingers armed with talons like eagles, large eyes of a fiery-red color, grisly hair streaming down his shoulders, iron boots, a pikestaff in his left hand, and a red cap on his head."[35]

The best-known tale of an encounter with a redcap is set in and around Hermitage Castle, near Newcastleton, in southern Scotland. Its owner in the early 1300s—a rich landowner named William de Soulis—was purportedly a sorcerer who conjured up evil spells that harmed various inhabitants of the region. One day, allegedly, he uttered magical words that made a redcap rise from its underground lair and terrorize residents of nearby farms and villages. The creature, which called itself Sly, seized children and offered their souls to the devil before eating them alive.

Eventually, the locals banded together, marched on de Soulis's mansion, and dragged him outside. There, they threw him into a big cauldron filled with boiling oil. And at the moment he died, the redcap fearfully retreated to its burrow, never to be seen again.

## Huge, Scaly Water Monsters

Far bigger and more destructive than kelpies or redcaps were oillipheists, enormous reptilian water monsters said to dwell in the Shannon River in central Ireland. "Like many dragons and

**oillipheist**
A large reptilian monster said to infest parts of Ireland's Shannon River

serpents in mythology," say the editors of the online site Mythical Creatures, an oillipheist is "portrayed as having a long, serpentine body covered in scales . . . [and] sharp claws and teeth, which it uses to capture prey or defend itself against attackers. . . . In some legends [an] oillipheist is said to have a gaze that can hypnotize or paralyze its victims, making them easy targets for its attacks."[36]

One of the best-known tales describes how one of these huge reptiles—Caoranach by name—came to be. According to the story, the famous Irish hero Finn MacCool and his Fenians were on a mission to slay an evil witch. As she tried to escape them, one of Finn's men fired an arrow, which struck and killed her. While the Fenians examined the body, a local man warned them not to break the witch's right thigh bone; thanks to a magic spell the old hag had conjured up, he explained, breaking that bone would unleash a terrible monster.

Later, a Fenian named Conan accidentally broke the bone, and out crawled a weird-looking worm. That small creature rapidly grew into the gigantic Caoranach, which went on a rampage and devoured nearly all the cattle in Ulster. Blaming himself for this calamity, Conan drew his sword, leaped into the beast's enormous mouth, and sliced the serpent to pieces from the inside.

For many centuries, the Celts of Ireland and the other British Isles believed that legendary beings like oillipheists, leprechauns, vampires, and redcaps were real. Myths about these strange creatures were "woven into tales whispered by firelight and guarded through generations of storytellers," says Keith O'Hara, an expert on Celtic Irish folklore. And even though people now know those beasts are only mythical, the tales about them remain popular. This, he points out, is because these creatures have "embodied the fears, hopes, and wonders of [the Celtic] people, from ancient times to modern day."[37]

# The Coming of Arthur

Long, long ago, in a lushly forested land called Cymru—today called Wales—a well-to-do Celtic landowner named Evrawc announced to his neighbors the birth of a son. The proud father added that he had named the boy Peredur. As the child grew, he displayed unusual strength, speed, and agility, as well as keen intelligence. He loved hiking and hunting in the woods, so his mother, Eliffer, often took him on outings in the large forest near the family mansion.

In that picturesque woodland, one day when the boy was in his teens, the mother and son unexpectedly encountered a group of men on horseback. Those riders were decked out in extensive armor and carried broadswords and lances, all of which hugely impressed Peredur. He greeted the strangers, who identified themselves as knights from Camelot. The wide-eyed young man had heard much about that magnificent castle, the hub of a small kingdom—also called Camelot—located somewhere to the east, in southern England. The ruler of that land, King Arthur, was renowned for his decency, fairness, and mission to protect the Celtic lands of the British Isles from outside invaders.

**Peredur**

In the Arthurian legends, a Welsh boy who journeys to Camelot, trains hard, and becomes the famous knight Sir Percival

The meeting in the woods that morning was like a dream come true for young Peredur. The idea of training to become one of Arthur's trusted knights had long fascinated him, and now—by an unbelievable stroke of luck—he had met several of those legendary warriors. They encouraged the young man to journey to Camelot and apply for such

*Peredur, later immortalized as Sir Percival, performed many legendary deeds, including slaying a monster serpent.*

special training. And the following year he did so. Arthur himself took an interest in him and was happy to bestow on him the prestigious title of Knight of the Round Table three years later.

It did not take Peredur long to distinguish himself as one of Camelot's most effective and widely admired warriors. The first notable deed for which he gained deserved fame occurred shortly after the widow of a well-to-do landowner sought him out and told him, "There are nine witches here!" Distraught, the woman said she needed help because "they have taken over and laid waste [to] the land."[38]

Peredur wasted no time in coming to the woman's aid. Arriving at her home, he saw one of the witches attacking a house servant. Swiftly, the young knight galloped over and used the hilt of his sword to strike the evil hag on the head. She momentarily escaped, but in the weeks that followed, Peredur, aided by another Arthurian knight, Sir Gwalchmai, slaughtered all nine witches. In time, this feat would prove to be only one of many legendary deeds Peredur would perform. Centuries later, the collected myths of the medieval Celts would immortalize him as one of Arthur's greatest knights—the steadfast and ethical Sir Percival.

## Tales from a Half-Forgotten Era

Although largely associated with English folklore, King Arthur, master of Camelot and leader of the so-called Knights of the Round Table, was first named in a ninth-century Welsh history of Britain. He is "a persistently iconic figure in medieval myths and histories," says Miranda Aldhouse-Green. "In the Welsh myths, he is associated with a curious mix of Christianity and pagan magic. God is frequently mentioned, but rubs shoulders with enchanted animals and magic cauldrons. . . . He is always presented as a larger-than-life, heroic figure, a champion fighter surrounded by gallant knights."[39]

Most of the Arthurian tales told and retold today, however, come from a cluster of late medieval European sources. These include English writer Geoffrey of Monmouth's *History of the Kings of Britain* (ca. 1136); *Le Morte d'Arthur* (*The Death of Arthur*, 1485) by another Englishman, Thomas Malory; and other assorted English, French, and German works of that period. These writings emerged within Europe's post-Celtic society. Yet they were based to a large degree on earlier Celtic narratives, most of which are now lost. And of the few surviving Celtic stories about Arthur, those from Wales are some of the most fascinating.

## The Lady of the Lake

The Arthurian legends are liberally sprinkled with fairies and other supernatural beings from the mystical universe depicted in the Celtic myths overall. One of the more memorable examples is the fairy queen at first called only the Lady of the Lake, but who later medieval writers gave the name Viviane. Supposedly she ruled a "queendom" lying beneath the surface of a large lake, a realm making up one of the several otherworlds of Celtic mythology. In the earliest stories about this watery dominion, its residents are both male and female, but later writings say it is populated only by women. In some medieval tales, the Lady of the Lake raised the young Lancelot, preparing him to be one of Arthur's knights. She also fashioned special weapons for both Lancelot and Arthur. The most famous example is Arthur's trusty sword Excalibur (called Caledfwlch in the Welsh versions of these stories). In one of the late medieval Arthurian tales, Viviane is depicted as one of the three fairy queens who, after the battle of Camlann, bears away the dying Arthur to a mystical land called Avalon.

Of particular importance for the Arthurian legends is the anonymous myth collection from which Peredur's stories come—the *Mabinogion*. It dates from about 1000 to 1100 CE. Yet it too was based on far earlier stories and legends, some of which go back to the era when the Celts battled the Romans, who occupied Britain in the first few centuries CE. And there are some researchers who believe Arthur may have been a historical figure from that tumultuous period of Roman Britain.

Thus, the original tales about Arthur and his knights come from the ancient period, rather than the medieval one. And to modern eyes, that makes those stories seem especially remote, quaint, magical, and otherworldly. In that storybook time and realm, British historian Richard Barber says, "We are in a world where the marvelous is normal, and where the laws of everyday life are suspended. The figures who inhabit this world are shapeshifters, possessors of strange skills, and are certainly the heirs of the ancient gods, if not the gods themselves."[40]

One thing is certain, Aldhouse-Green points out: Despite originating in a far corner of Europe in a distant, half-forgotten era, the

Arthurian myths eventually gained nothing less than universal renown. "The living, historical figure of Arthur," she writes, "inspired a whole constellation of stories about medieval chivalry, heroism, and consummate fighting skill that spanned not only Wales but also the whole of Britain and [the entire world] beyond."[41]

## Real? Or Only a Dream?

One shining star in that constellation of old tales in the *Mabinogion* has a clever, almost modern-style twist. Titled *The Dream of Rhonabwy*, it deals with a twelfth-century Welsh knight who fell asleep and dreamed he had traveled centuries backward in time to the era of King Arthur. As the myth begins, Rhonabwy and two companions were ordered by their king to track down the leader of a failed rebellion, and on the third day of the search, while in a forest, the three encountered a severe storm. Fortunately for them, they found a house whose owner, a hermit, allowed them to stay the night.

**Rhonabwy**
**A Welsh warrior who dreams he goes back several centuries and meets the famous King Arthur**

After falling asleep, Rhonabwy had a highly realistic and vivid dream in which he and his companions were riding through eastern Wales. But he had a disquieting feeling because the countryside seemed somewhat different than what he was used to. For instance, one hill that was normally covered by trees was now treeless. Also, from the summit of that hill, Rhonabwy could see an enormous castle in the distance, a structure he did not recognize.

While trying to decide whether to approach the castle, the three men saw an armor-clad horseman approaching them at tremendous speed. Assuming they were under attack, they galloped away, but the rider soon caught up to them. "Mercy! Mercy!"[42] Rhonabwy cried out, according to Arthurian researcher Jeffrey Wikstrom. Thinking that the weapons-laden rider was a far greater warrior than they, the three immediately surrendered.

Hearing that, the rider laughed heartily and said there was no need to surrender. He was pursuing them only to bring a message.

"I am Iddawc ap Mynyo," he said, "but you can call me Sir Corth, as that's the name by which I'm best-known."[43] The message, he went on, was from King Arthur, master of yonder castle, Camelot. At present, Corth explained, Arthur was preparing his army to fight a force of invaders near Mount Badon.

These words left Rhonabwy and his companions quite confused because they were under the impression that Arthur had been dead for several centuries. Nevertheless, they followed Corth, who brought them to the king's camp, on the banks of the Severn River. Wikstrom writes that "it would have taken an hour to walk around [the huge camp], so full and large was it. Tents and camp-

*Rhonabwy dreamed he had traveled centuries backward in time to the era of King Arthur (depicted here), an iconic figure who was master of Camelot and leader of the Knights of the Round Table.*

## Who Was King Arthur?

Was Arthur purely a mythical character? Or was he a real person, and if so, who was he? Over the centuries, these questions have haunted mythologists and other scholars, as well as millions of ordinary people. Modern experts have advanced several theories, each attempting to identify a historical Arthur. Although none are yet universally accepted, the one that has so far drawn the most attention, scholarly and otherwise, suggests that the mythical Arthur was based on a Romano-Celtic military leader. After controlling Britain for over three centuries, in the early 400s Rome abandoned it. Many of the natives—culturally a blend of Roman and Celt—remained. And they were soon threatened by tribal peoples from western Europe. A courageous cavalry commander bearing the Roman title or rank of Artorius led the defense against the intruders. *Arthur* is the Welsh rendering of the Latin *Artorius*. The chief proponents of this theory are noted Arthurian scholars Linda A. Malcor and C. Scott Littleton. They hold that that cavalry commander and his stalwart horsemen, or knights, scored enough victories that they became legendary to later generations of Britons. The atmospheric 2004 film *King Arthur*, starring Clive Owen in the title role, was based in large degree on Malcors and Littleton's theory.

fires and cabins and lots of shouting. At the edge of the camp, on a low island out on the Severn, Rhonabwy met King Arthur."[44]

At first, Arthur seemed interested in who the three strangers were. But then, seemingly for no good reason, he suddenly ignored them while he played chess with one of his knights. While Rhonabwy politely waited, some trumpets blared, indicating that the enemy army was approaching. At this, Arthur hurried toward his soldiers, and at that moment the dream abruptly ended. The dreamer found himself in the hermit's house in the forest. It seemed to Rhonabwy that the entire episode with Corth and Arthur had taken only a couple of hours. But the hermit informed him that he had been asleep for three days and three nights. To his dying day, Rhonabwy wondered whether it had been only a dream or whether, through some sort of magic, he had gone back and met the great King Arthur.

## Enormous Worldwide Popularity

Rhonabwy's tale and the other stories contained in the *Mabinogion* account for only a small portion of the myths about Arthur and Camelot that arose during the medieval era. With each passing century, new tales or elaborations of older ones proliferated throughout the British Isles and beyond. Some describe adventures and quests by various Knights of the Round Table. Especially popular among these is the search for the so-called Holy Grail (in Welsh the *Greal Sanctaidd*); initially, it was portrayed as a magical stone but was later said to be the cup Jesus used at the Last Supper. Several of Arthur's knights supposedly hunted for it, including Percival, Lancelot, and Galahad. In the end, Galahad found the Grail and thereafter ascended into heaven.

**Galahad**
**One of Arthur's best-known knights, he searched for and found the magical relic known as the Holy Grail**

Many other medieval Arthurian myths deal with Arthur's family troubles. Prominent among these is the affair his wife, Queen Guinevere, has with Sir Lancelot and how Arthur's son, Mordred, becomes an enemy of the king and Camelot. Noted Arthurian scholars C. Scott Littleton and Linda A. Malcor briefly summarize how these varied storylines eventually merge and lead to the fall of Camelot:

> Adultery, betrayal, treason, and civil war are interwoven in the tragic tale of Arthur's death. With the failure of so many of the knights to finish or even to return from the quest for the Grail, Arthur was all but defenseless when the evil Mordred arranged to catch Lancelot alone with Guinevere and expose their affair. The events that followed led inevitably to the final battle of Camlann [fought between the armies of Arthur and Mordred], and ultimately to Arthur's death at the hands of Mordred.[45]

The later enormous worldwide popularity of the Arthurian legends, the most renowned of the Celtic myths, speaks for itself.

*Lancelot, at left, fights another knight to defend the honor of Guinevere.*

Arthur, his brave knights, and the noble ideals they fought for live on today in countless books, films, television shows, graphic novels, video games, and other forms of entertainment. This fact clearly demonstrates one of the most profound aspects of Celtic myths. Namely, their characters, concepts, and plots are not only immensely entertaining but also thought provoking in the way they explore the complex connections between human society and the natural world. As Littleton and Malcor put it, the Arthurian stories, and by extension the Celtic myths as a whole, "are a celebration of what humans can create and a lamentation [sad expression] for what they destroy. They span the gap from Celtic times to the present, each new generation finding something fascinating and inspiring in these timeless tales."[46]

## Introduction: Who Were the Celts?


1. Fergus Fleming, "Battles of the Heroes," in Time-Life Books, *Heroes of the Dawn*. London: Duncan Baird, 1996, p. 51.
2. Quoted in Elizabeth A. Gray, trans., "The Second Battle of Mag Tuired," Sacred Texts. https://sacred-texts.com.
3. Quoted in Gray, "The Second Battle of Mag Tuired."
4. Fleming, "The Celtic World," p. 9.
5. Fleming, "The Celtic World," p. 12.


## Chapter One: Tales of Beginnings


6. Barry Cunliffe. *The Celts: A Very Short Introduction*. New York: Oxford University Press, 2003, p. 56.
7. Philip Freeman, *Celtic Mythology*. New York: Oxford University Press, 2017, p. 16.
8. Quoted in Lady Gregory, *Gods and Fighting Men: The Story of the Tuatha De Danaan and of the Fianna of Ireland*. London: John Murray, 1910, pp. xviii–xix.
9. Arthur Cotterell, *Celtic Mythology*. New York: Lorenz, 1999, p. 22.
10. James Harpur, *Celtic Myth: A Treasury of Legends*, *Art, and History*. New York: Sharpe, 2008, pp. 28–29.
11. Peter B. Ellis, *Celtic Myths and Legends*. New York: Carroll and Graf, 2006, p. 20.


## Chapter Two: Epic Stories of Lovers


12. Fleming, "Battles of the Heroes," p. 70.
13. Fleming, "Battles of the Heroes," p. 70.
14. Robert Seutter, "Celtic Love—Nothing Short of Epic!," True Thomas the Storyteller. http://truethomas.com.
15. Freeman, *Celtic Mythology*, p. 37.
16. Sam McBratney, *Celtic Myths*. New York: Bedrick, 1997, p. 55.
17. Quoted in Ellis, *Celtic Myths and Legends*, p. 374.
18. Quoted in Ellis, *Celtic Myths and Legends*, p. 383.
19. Ellis, *Celtic Myths and Legends*, p. 397.
20. Charles Squire, *Celtic Myth and Legend*. Franklin Lakes, NJ: Career, 2001, p. 184.


## Chapter Three: The Great Celtic Heroes


21. Quoted in Freeman, *Celtic Mythology*, p. 30.
22. Quoted in Freeman, *Celtic Mythology*, p. 31.
23. Quoted in Freeman, *Celtic Mythology*, p. 31.

24. Freeman, *Celtic Mythology*, p. 31.
25. Aimee Vipond, "The Heroic Ballads of the Celtic Kings," Celtic Mythology, November 10, 2024. https://celtic.mythologyworldwide.com.
26. Christopher R. Fee, *Gods, Heroes, and Kings: The Battle for Mythic Britain*. New York: Oxford University Press, 2004, p. 191.
27. McBratney, *Celtic Myths*, pp. 13–14.
28. Quoted in McBratney, *Celtic Myths*, p. 14.
29. Quoted in Thomas Kinsella, trans., *The Tain*. Oxford: Oxford University Press, 2002, pp. 150–52.
30. Squire, *Celtic Myth and Legend*, pp. 203–4.
31. Anne Ross, *Druids, Gods, and Heros from Celtic Mythology*. New York: Bedrick, 1986, p. 62.

## Chapter Four: Strange Creatures and Scary Monsters

32. Miranda Aldhouse-Green, *The Celic Myths*. London: Thames and Hudson, 2015, pp. 22–23.
33. Cierra Tolentino, "Celtic Mythology: Myths, Legends, Deities, Heroes, and Culture," History Cooperative, October 29, 2024. https://historycooperative.org.
34. Jane Wilde, *Ancient Legends, Mystic Charms, and Superstitions of Ireland*, vol. 1. Boston: Ticknor, 1887, pp. 259–60.
35. William Henderson, *Notes on the Folklore of the Northern Counties of England and the Borders*. London: Satchell, 1879, p. 253.
36. Mythical Creatures, "Oillipheist," 2025. https://mythical-creatures.com.
37. Keith O'Hara, "30 Irish Mythological Creatures and Their Legends," Irish Road Trip, November 8, 2024. www.theirishroadtrip.com.

## Chapter Five: The Coming of Arthur

38. Quoted in Gwyn Jones and Thomas Jones, trans., *The Mabinogion*. London: Dent, 1974, p. 10.
39. Aldhouse-Green, *The Celtic Myths*, pp. 95–96.
40. Richard Barber, *Myths and Legends of the British Isles*. New York: Barnes and Noble, 2004, p. xi.
41. Aldhouse-Green, *The Celtic Myths*, p. 97.
42. Quoted in Jeffrey Wikstrom, "Primary Sources: The Mabinogion, 'The Dream of Rhonabwy,' Complete in One Post," Primary Sources, April 9, 2015. www.jeffwik.com.
43. Quoted in Wikstrom, "Primary Sources."
44. Wikstrom, "Primary Sources."
45. C. Scott Littleton and Linda A. Malcor, "The Fall of Camelot," in Time-Life Books, *Heroes of the Dawn*. London: Duncan Baird, 1996, p. 132.
46. Littleton and Malcor, "Legends of Arthur," in Time-Life Books, *Heroes of the Dawn*. London: Duncan Baird, 1996, p. 103.

## Books

Ethan Craftwell, *Celtic Mythology for Beginners*. Self-published, 2024.

John Farrelly, *The Celts*. Dublin, Ireland: O'Brien, 2020.

Mark Joyce, *Mythical Irish Beasts*. Dublin, Ireland: Currach, 2024.

Him Sapiro, *Celtic Mythology Explained for Kids*. Denver, CO: Ched, 2021.

Billy Wellman, *Celts for Kids*. Self-published, 2024.

Billy Wellman, *Irish Mythology*. Self-published, 2024.

## Internet Sources

BBC, "Culhwch and Olwen," 2014. www.bbc.co.uk.

Britain Express, "Tales of the Mabinogion." www.britainexpress.com.

Nicholas Collender, "Celtic Legends of Romance," Irish Trees, 2025. https://irishtrees.ie.

Ciaran Connolly, "Incredible History of the Tuatha de Danann: Ireland's Most Ancient Race," Connolly Cove, May 20, 2024. www.connollycove.com.

Zteve T. Evans, "Ancient Celtic Cauldrons: The Magical, the Mythical, the Real," Folklore Thursday, February 11, 2021. https://folklorethursday.com.

Joshua Hammer, "Was King Arthur a Real Person?," *Smithsonian*, September 1, 2022. www.smithsonianmag.com.

Irish Myths, "What Is Irish Mythology?" https://irishmyths.com.

Aimee Vipond, "The Heroic Ballads of the Celtic Kings," Celtic Mythology, November 10, 2024. https://celtic.mythologyworldwide.com.

Graham Watkins, "Welsh Legends and Myths: King Arthur." www.grahamwatkins.info.

Michael Wood. "King Arthur, 'Once and Future King,'" BBC, February 17, 2011. www.bbc.co.uk.

## Websites

**History Cooperative, Celtic Mythology: Myths, Legends, Deities, Heroes, and Culture**
https://historycooperative.org/celtic-mythology
This enormous, very useful website contains dozens of links to specific gods, creatures, and heroes, as well as to articles about ancient Celtic religion and summaries of the key myths.

**The Irish Road Trip**
www.theirishroadtrip.com
By typing "Celtic mythology" into the search bar, visitors to this online Ireland travel guide can find links to a variety of articles about those myths and about the gods and goddesses of ancient Celtic culture.

**Mythopedia, Ultimate Guide to Celtic Mythology**
https://mythopedia.com/guides/celtic-mythology
The editors of the reliable Mythopedia websites offer this handy guide to the chief Celtic gods. Each biography of a god contains numerous links to related stories and topics.

**Wilderness Ireland, The Folklore of Ireland**
www.wildernessireland.com/folklore-of-ireland
The popular Irish adventure tour company Wilderness Ireland sponsors this extensive, well-researched collection of articles about Celtic Irish legends and myths. Numerous links lead to related articles about various gods, heroes, creatures, and more.

Cover: Shutterstock AI Generator

6: Bridgeman Images
9: ARTGEN /Alamy Stock Photo
10: Alamy Stock Photo
12: Art Directors & TRIP/Alamy Stock Photo
20: Florilegius/Alamy Stock Photo
22: Chronicle/Alamy Stock Photo
26: The Stapleton Collection/Bridgeman Images
28: Florilegius/Newscom
32: Chronicle/Alamy Stock Photo
35: Chronicle/Alamy Stock Photo
38: Charles Walker Collection/Alamy Stock Photo
43: North Wind Picture Archives/Alamy Stock Photo
44: Dusan Kostic/Alamy Stock Photo
48: Charles Walker Collection/Alamy Stock Photo
52: Ivy Close Images/Alamy Stock Photo
55: Chronicle/Alamy Stock Photo

## ABOUT THE AUTHOR

Classical historian and award-winning author Don Nardo has written numerous acclaimed volumes about ancient civilizations and peoples. They include more than four dozen overviews of the mythologies of the Sumerians, Babylonians, Egyptians, Greeks, Romans, Persians, Celts, Chinese, Aztecs, Hindus, Native Americans, and others. Nardo, who also composes and arranges orchestral music, lives with his wife, Christine, in Massachusetts.